C000137388

ST ANDREWS & NORTH-EAST FIFE'S BUSES

WALTER BURT

AMBERLEY PUBLISHING

Acknowledgements

Once again, I am indebted to the following people for allowing me to use their fantastic images to illustrate this book. Without them, the rich variety of images would not exist and would make for some dull reading. I make no apologies for using the photographs of so many individuals. This has been necessary due to the difficulties I have found in trying to research the history of a limited amount of vehicles. In no particular order, my heartfelt thanks go to John Sinclair, Innes Cameron, Brian McDevitt, Dr George Fairbairn, Andy Wood, Robert Dickson, Len Wright, Roger Norton, John Law, Barry Sanjana, Peter Relf collection, Andrew Cook, Richard Huggins, Clive A. Brown, Gordon Stirling, Malcolm Audsley, Gary Seamarks, Patrick Castelli, Ewan Wood, Suzy Scott, Chris Cuthill, Robert Clark, Michael Laing.

First published 2013

Amberley Publishing
The Hill, Stroud
Gloucestershire, GL5 4EP

www.amberley-books.com

ISBN 978 1 4456 1648 3
E-Book ISBN 978 1 4456 1667 4

British Library Cataloguing in Publication Data.
A catalogue record for this book is available from the British Library.

Typeset in 9.5pt on 12pt Celeste.
Typesetting by Amberley Publishing.
Printed in the UK.

Introduction

It has been quite a journey for me and it is going to come to an end with this book. This area of Fife was not blessed with large towns with their own tramway systems, or any sort of large urban areas where there were numerous amounts of entrepreneurs starting up a bus service in competition with like-minded individuals. No, the horse-drawn carriage lasted a little bit longer up in the north and east Neuk than it did in the more industrial west and central areas of Fife.

Because of the rural nature of the location covered, it has proved very difficult to find images, particularly of the vehicles used throughout the area prior to the Walter Alexander days. I would also have liked to have included a wider variety of vehicles, but again, due to the rural location, the number of buses used by the various depots was quite minimal compared to the depots in the west and central parts of Fife. This has resulted in many of the vehicles appearing more than once in the book; a fact of which I hope does not spoil it for the reader and enthusiast alike. Nevertheless, the images I have drawn from the various collections of all my good friends, have hopefully provided an insight into the way the buses have operated in this area through the years.

As those of you who have read my other bus books will already know, it is my practice to include the registration and fleet numbers of the vehicles in the photographs. I usually also try to include the chassis type and body manufacturer, although I understand it can be a bit repetitive to read. This is done in case people want to use a specific image and its description, when using this book for their own research purposes. Also, it can be quite confusing to some people when the same type of body work can appear on more than one chassis type, as often happens within these pages. Vehicles have also appeared more than once when the main Fife Company have re-numbered their fleet in readiness for privatisation, and when Stagecoach bought the company in 1991.

Brief History

The north and north-eastern region of Fife has always been a rural area due to its isolation before the opening of the Tay railway bridge in 1878, (and subsequent bridges). Travellers had always tended to travel from the southern end of the county to Perth via the Great North Road, or on one of the coastal sea services operating at the time.

Cupar was the county town in Fife and was one of the first areas to benefit from new road building programmes during the late eighteenth and early nineteenth centuries. During the following two or three decades, many of the other larger towns in the region were being connected to this new road network, which helped to improve communication and movement within the local towns and villages.

It was not until after the First World War that new operators began to run bus services due to the availability of surplus vehicles and chassis from the military. There were not too many of these adventurous pioneers in this part of Fife, it just wasn't as large a populated region as the southern and central parts of the county were. Perhaps the major pioneer of bus services in the north and east of Fife was Tom Gardner, who started operating services from a garage at Harbour head, Anstruther, in the mid 1920s. His proved to be a successful venture, and so required a larger garage. A new purpose built garage was erected in Pittenweem Road on the southern side of the town, and this garage was the one that eventually passed into Alexander (Fife) hands and was subsequently closed by Fife Scottish Omnibuses in 1981. This depot features quite prominently within the pages of this book. He ran buses on a route from Anstruther to St Andrews via Crail which extended within a couple of years to become Leven to Newport via the coast. This was the forerunner of the service 355, later to become service 95 which is still operated by Stagecoach Fife to this day. He also started operating on a route from Anstruther to St Andrews via Dunino which became service 361 after Alexander's took over his operation in 1932.

It was not until 1923, when the General Motor Carrying Company Ltd (GMC) of Kirkcaldy started to run bus services in the St Andrews area that things really started to happen. Buses were apparently driven up in the mornings and back down to their Kirkcaldy depot each night until a depot was opened in the same year by the GMC in Grange Road, in the golfing town. They operated services initially from St Andrews to Anstruther via Crail from 1923 and three years later on a similar service via Kingsbarns. A second service was started in 1928 which ran to Cupar via Blebo.

Cupar, being the County Town of Fife, and also its administrative centre, could boast three serious bus operators in the area. The first of these operators is Grant's Bus Service. He had originally been operating horse-drawn carriages from stables at the towns Cupar Arms Hotel until he purchased his first charabanc around 1920. All his routes originated from Cupar and reached out to St. Andrews via Dairsie and Guardbridge; Newport and Ladybank. He also ran some Saturday only routes to Springfield; Logie and Luthrie via Rathillet. His operations were acquired by Alexander's in 1930, but the services were operated by another of Alexander's subsidiaries, Simpson's & Forrester's.

The next serious bus operator in Cupar was Central Garage. They operated from a base at Cupar Crossgate which was to remain in use as a bus garage until it too was closed by Fife

Scottish Omnibuses in 1981. Apparently this prime site is now the location of a supermarket in the town. The company started off purely as a garage business selling motor fuel and servicing. In a similar story to Grant's as I have already mentioned, Central Garage bought their first charabanc in 1920 and used it for touring work. It was not until three years later (1923) that they started doing stage carrying work based around Cupar. They ran similar type of routes to those run by Grant's, including the lucrative route to the ferry terminal at Newport. It is reported that both Central Garage and Grant's bus services had been indulging in the type of bus piracy that was happening on other routes in the central and southern parts of Fife. The Central Garage Company was purchased in 1930 by the Scottish Motor Transport group and control of their operations was also passed to the Simpson's & Forrester's company.

The third undertaking to emerge in Cupar was that of Sharp's Motors. Like the previous two undertakings, Sharp's ran service originating from Cupar and travelled to Springfield via Stratheden, Elie via Peat Inn, Largowood and Colinsburgh, and finally to Ladybank then Kingskettle. The Ladybank route was operated with competition from Grant's Bus Service. It is also reported that Sharp's may have been the subject of a takeover by the Central Garage Company

Other operators in this area included Clow's Motors of Guardbridge. They operated on the lucrative service between St Andrews and the Newport Ferry via Guardbridge and Leuchars. Apparently, the route was ultimately shared with the GMC and they had arranged to meet alternate ferries. Clow's was acquired by the ever growing Walter Alexander Company in 1935.

Another operator to the north of the county was Fullers Motors of Newburgh. Initially a taxi operator, they began running a service from Newburgh to Perth about 1922. This route later became St Andrews – Newburgh – Perth via Strathmiglo. They also ran to Markinch via Falkland. They were purchased by the GMC of Kirkcaldy, and although Fullers continued to run their services more or less independently, the GMC used Fullers Garage to house some of their vehicles. I think this garage may have ended up as Newburgh depot, which although closed in 1991, still remains as an outstation – similar to what the GMC were using it for I suppose.

Johnstones was another operator from north Fife operating from a base in Tayport, initially on a service to and from the Newport Ferry. He also ran a service to St Andrews from 1930 and was acquired by Alexander in 1935.

The final main operator in this area was Robertsons, who operated from Gauldry Main Street. This company started as a taxi operator and also did school contract work. They too, had an involvement on the Newport Ferry service and ran from Gauldry at weekends only. They were sold to Williamson of Gauldry after the Second World War, who themselves merged with Moffat of Cardenden in 1978 to become the Moffat & Williamson Company still in existence today. Some of the vehicles of Williamson, and of the merged Moffat & Williamson companies are featured in these pages too.

It was also during the nineteenth century that the marvel that was the railway began to make inroads into the county. This was a great benefit to the farmers and traders in the area as it help with the movement of goods and livestock that could previously only have been done on a small scale. During the twentieth century though, when the infamous Dr Beeching started wielding his railway axe, this area of Fife lost practically its entire rural network, retaining only the part of the east coast main line running through this part of the county. It was then, that the bus services in the area started to benefit from the increase in passengers who would have previously used the rail network. In more recent times, tentative efforts have been raised in trying to get the golfing centre of St Andrews re-connected to the railway system. All efforts have continually failed, but perseverance is a must, and if it can happen to the small town of Alloa, I am sure it can happen at the home of golf too. The many thousands that flock to St Andrews when a major competition is underway rely on the numerous buses that are used to transfer passengers between the town and the nearest railway station at Leuchars.

Let us not overlook the part played by the Post Office in serving the most rural of area in our magnificent county. Although not shown in earlier timetables, I know that the Post Office operated vehicles for use as a lifeline for those in need of its services. I won't list the 'in between' places as they are too numerous, although just as important. The main services were as follows:

• Service No.10 ran from Cupar Post Office to Peat Inn and back. (11 Seater)
• Service No.27 ran from Anstruther to Arncroach and back. (11 Seater)
• Service No.52 ran from Leven to New Gilston and back. (11 Seater)
• Service No.91 ran from Dollar to Glendevon and back. (4 Seater)
• Service No.94 ran from Kinross to Rumbling Bridge and back. (11 Seater)

There were also another five Cupar-based local rural runs going to and from Kilmany/Birkhill, Brunton, Kilmany/Brunton, Newburgh and Newburgh via Letham.
I know very little about how the Post Office services were organised or operated, only that, as I have already stated, they must have been a lifeline for certain people in the places that buses couldn't or didn't reach.

The population in this part of Fife is growing too, and it will not be too long before towns like St Andrews will be requiring bigger bus stations. Although the area might not require the building of any further depots as such, perhaps the day will come soon when a larger depot may need to be built, to replace the rather limited confines of the combined depot and bus station at St Andrews at present.

Now that this book is done, I hope I have shown how the buses and trams that have operated throughout our Kingdom of Fife, have all fitted together to become what is today the bus operations of Stagecoach Fife

FG2301 was a Karrier belonging to Central Garage of Cupar who ran a handful of local services from the town. This vehicle is seen outside its home depot in Crossgate before heading off on a run to Falkland in the late 1920s.

Another early bus can be seen parked outside the town hall at Crail. The image is not very sharp and clear, but the vehicle may be a Thornycroft belonging to one of a few bus companies that operated through the town on their way to or from St Andrews.

Upper Largo is the location of another early type of bus as it picks up a passenger on a local service running through the village. It wouldn't be unjust to compare Upper Largo to a ghost town in this early post card image.

When you see an image like this with only a bus and a van on view, it is easy to understand why people relied on public transport so much. Quite simply, unless you were prepared to walk, there were no other options available. This late 1930s view shows WG4452 (P338), an Alexander's TS7 ready to leave on a local service from Falkland Palace.

BMS592 (G70) is ready to depart from its home depot and bus stance, in the coastal town of St Andrews. It is a Guy Arab 3 with body work by Massey, and was new to Walter Alexander in 1948. It is presumably on a 'part route' run to Cupar as the service 23 ran from St Andrews to Glasgow. *(John Sinclair)*

Included in this line-up at Cupar depot in the early 1950s, we find on the left, FG9428 (P478), a Leyland Tiger with Alexander bodywork acquired from Simpson's and Forrester's in 1938. Next on the right is CWG57 (RB79) a Leyland PD2/1, again with Alexander's own bodywork.

AFG416 was a Leyland LT5A numbered as N242 in the fleet of the General Motor Carrying Company of Kirkcaldy before that company was purchased in 1937 by Walter Alexander. It was renumbered as P701 after being re-engined in 1945 and is seen here in the environs of St Andrews bus depot. It was withdrawn in 1957 and sold to Penders Circus of Edinburgh but was last licensed in 1960. *(John Sinclair)*

New in 1948, AWG566 (G52) was a Guy Arab 3 with a Brockhouse body seating thirty-five passengers. Withdrawn in 1966, it would find itself in the scrapheap at Muir's in Kirkcaldy by the end of the year. The location looks like St Andrews which would be correct if the service number is 364, which I believe it to be, as this is the St Andrews to Perth service. *(John Sinclair)*

You will find that this service number is one that will crop up often in this book. It seems that is was a frequent and long journey that used a lot of vehicles. This image shows Alexander-bodied Leyland Tiger Cub GWG274 (PD48) of Anstruther depot, sitting on stance at St Andrews ready for the next leg of its journey down the Fife coast to Leven. New in 1955, it was finally withdrawn from service in 1972 and ended up at Muir's in Kirkcaldy. *(John Sinclair)*

Another of the Alexander-bodied Tiger Cubs, GWG296 (PD70), is pictured here sitting on stance, again at St Andrews bus station. This is a good illustration that shows the layout of the rear end of the vehicle, and also shows how the Alexander name was applied to the boot area. *(John Sinclair)*

St Andrews depot is once more the focus of attention, as what looks like a Burlingham-bodied Leyland LZ2A is seen sitting broadside on to the photographer. This is a good illustration for showing how the body side styling was applied around the wheel arches and the waist of the vehicle. You will also see here how little the Bluebird emblem has changed over the years. *(John Sinclair)*

I have previously used this image in the Kirkcaldy area book, wrongly describing the location as Kirkcaldy bus station. I now know that it is St Andrews and that the bus, a 1935 Alexander-bodied Leyland LT5A, is in fact on the service 355 from Dundee and heading towards Leven. WG3260 (P705) was withdrawn in 1959, but saw further use with Williamson of Gauldry until 1963 when it was sold on and used as a caravan until 1979. *(John Sinclair)*

Another rear end illustration is included here as it depicts another style of body from the previous rear end offering. WG3260 (P705) was new to Alexander's in 1935 and originally carried the fleet number N230 but was renumbered in 1945 after being re-engined. This bus was also withdrawn in 1959 but saw further use with another three Fife-based owners before being used for spares for other preserved vehicles. *(John Sinclair)*

WG9502 (P666) was one of the Alexander-bodied Leyland TS8 specials that arrived in Fife in 1940 with the Alexander company. It is pictured here at the drop off area at St Andrews bus station on the service 355 to Leven. Although a tiny bit blurred, the bus would probably have been an Anstruther-based machine. This vehicle saw twenty-three year's service in Fife before heading off to Muir's scrapyard in Kirkcaldy long known to be the graveyard for many of Fifes buses. *(John Sinclair)*

We find ourselves at Cupar depot as we catch AWG568 (G54), awaiting its next turn of duty on a dull and wet day sometime in the late 1950s. It is another Guy Arab 3, but with bodywork by Brockhouse. Withdrawn from service in late 1966, it was sold to Muir's in March the following year. *(Innes Cameron Collection)*

St Andrews was always a popular destination, not just for holidaymakers but for tour buses too. A good selection of vehicles from other areas could always be seen during the summer months. A good example is shown here by WG7260 (K28) a Burlingham-bodied Leyland LZ2A from Kelty depot and EMS534 (PC79) an Alexander (Midland) Leyland Royal Tiger from Balfron depot. *(John Sinclair)*

WG8261 (R242) was a Leyland Titan TD5 with Leyland's own bodywork. It is pictured, I believe, at Cupar depot. It is obviously another one of the many vehicles used on the service 364 between Perth and St Andrews. New in 1939, it would be withdrawn in 1961 and sold on to Thomson of Glasgow. *(John Sinclair)*

This postcard image shows us two vehicles belonging to Walter Alexander parked up in South Street in the town of St Andrews. South Street was used as a departure point for some of the services serving the town. I am not too sure what type of buses these are supposed to represent, but I will leave it up to the individual to decide.

7436SP (FW4) was a unique vehicle in the Fife fleet as it was the only one of the five Bedford VAS1s operated which had a Duple Midland bus body (B30F layout). The other four vehicles had the C29F type of bodies by Duple. It is seen when new in 1962, allocated to Newburgh depot, before being repainted into Fife's Ayres red livery. This bus was withdrawn in 1972, eventually ending up two years later working for Henihane, an operator in Galway. *(John Sinclair)*

Newburgh depot allocated Leyland Tiger Cub OMS252 (PD176) is seen between turns on the service 364 which ran between St Andrews and Perth via Cupar and Newburgh. The deeper front grille is evident on this 1960 Alexander-bodied example seen sitting in St Andrews.

FW4 is once again the subject as it is seen here nearer the mid-1960s in its newer Ayres red colour scheme. At this point in time, it can be seen to be still allocated to Newburgh, At one time Fife's most northerly dedicated bus depot. *(John Sinclair)*

In July 1967, DMS820 (FPB7), a sixteen-year-old Leyland Tiger OPS2/1 with Alexander coach body style, is seen to be taking a break at Tayport Railway Station on the 355 service. This service ran between Leven and Newport and ran via St Andrews down the coast. This bus was withdrawn in 1970 and eventually ended up restored and preserved, last being reported at Lathalmond near Dunfermline.

DWG525 (FPC29) was a Leyland Royal Tiger, built with their in-house style of body work. This bus has had replacement indicators fitted as they were originally fitted with a 'semaphore' type of trafficator. The location of the old trafficator can be seen by the narrow vertical panel strip near the front off-side of the vehicle. This vehicle was withdrawn and sold to a dealership in Preston in 1970. *(John Sinclair)*

Fife's only bus-bodied Bedford VAS1 is once again included in the subject matter when seen inside Cupar depot, where it was allocated to in the last few years of service with Fife. In the ten years it served within Fife, because it was classed as a small vehicle, it ran as one-man operated. Its companion on the left DMS818 (FPB5), another 1951 Leyland Tiger with Alexander bodywork, was converted to PS1 standard in 1960 using parts from withdrawn PS1s. *(John Sinclair)*

Anstruther bus depot is the location as we find yet another Leyland Tiger, DMS829 (FPB16), which had been converted to PS1 standard in 1960. Its stable mate is BMS214 (FPA52), one of the original PS1 Leyland Tigers. Both buses have Alexander's bodywork and were both withdrawn in 1969. FPB16 went to Muir's in Kirkcaldy whilst FPA52 was sold to Lendrick Muir School by Rumbling Bridge, Kinross. *(John Sinclair)*

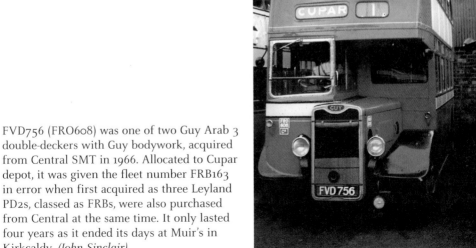

FVD756 (FRO608) was one of two Guy Arab 3 double-deckers with Guy bodywork, acquired from Central SMT in 1966. Allocated to Cupar depot, it was given the fleet number FRB163 in error when first acquired as three Leyland PD2s, classed as FRBs, were also purchased from Central at the same time. It only lasted four years as it ended its days at Muir's in Kirkcaldy. *(John Sinclair)*

FRO608 is once again the subject here as we have a look at the rear styling of the Guy bodywork. The styling of the lining was much suited to Guy's bodywork as can be seen while parked up within the confines of its home depot at Cupar. *(John Sinclair)*

FRO608 can once again be seen in this line up at Cupar a year or so after the images previously. It can be seen in the company of its fellow former Central SMT Guy Arab 3, FVD757 (FRO609), on the left. The central vehicle is CWG49 (FRB71), a Leyland PD2/1 with Alexander bodywork which was bought new in 1950 by the Fife area operation. Like many others of this vintage, it was withdrawn in 1970 and sold for scrap to Muir's in March the following year. The aluminium sliding window frames can be clearly seen here on the Guy-bodied vehicles. *(John Sinclair)*

Another of the 1950 batch of Leyland PD2/1s was CWG50 (FRB72). This is a good study of the platform area of one of the Alexander-bodied vehicles and doesn't look too dissimilar to the Guy bodywork at the time. This bus was also withdrawn in 1970 but had a brief spell as a service vehicle (Driver Trainer) number T2, a photograph of which can be seen on page 92 of the *Fife Buses* book by the author. *(John Sinclair)*

355 would appear to be the dominant service that Anstruther supplied buses for, as witnessed in this late 1960s scene. We see a sort of reversed evolution of Alexander bus types here as AEC Reliance GXA154D (FAC54), on the left, has the stylish new Alexander Y-type of bodywork in the reversed colours of the coach livery. Next is DMS829 (FPB16), another of the Leyland Tigers converted to PS1 standard in 1960, and lastly on the right is BMS214 (FPA52), one of the original 1948 PS1s. *(John Sinclair)*

Once again, one of the original Leyland PS1s with Alexander bodywork was BMS211 (FPA49). This was one allocated to Newburgh depot and can be witnessed on the arduous service 336 between Kirkcaldy and Perth via Newburgh and Falkland. As it is a Newburgh-based vehicle, I can only surmise it was on one of the short workings between its home town and 'The Fair City' of Perth.

How to make something ugly, even uglier – just paint it in the most unimaginative version of the company livery. I am no lover of the Albion Lowlander, as you may know from previous books, but at least Alexander tried to redress the upstairs seating issue on later batches of their bodywork for this type of vehicle. The nearside front canopy was lowered to allow the upstairs front seating to be more or less in keeping with the rest of the upper saloon. UCS624 (FRE39) was one of St Andrews allocation and is seen within the bus station area in the town. *(Brian McDevitt)*

UCS624 (FRE39) is shown again, but this time it is parked up outside the main shed and, as I have pointed out in my other books, this image displays how clean the buses were kept when under the control of Alexander (Fife). Similar to the other depots in the north and east of Fife, the dominant service seems to be the 355 which ran between Leven and Newport or Dundee after the Tay Road Bridge opened. *(Innes Cameron Collection)*

RWG375 (FRD152), shown in the middle of this trio, was an LD6G type Lodekka and was one of the last buses ordered by Walter Alexander before the company split in 1961. It was delivered in May of that year but did not enter service until after the formation of the Alexander (Fife) company. It is flanked by two interlopers in the shape of GM7006 (FRD101) and GM7001 (FRD105). These two arrived in 1969 when fourteen years old from Central SMT and are seen within the confines of Cupar depot. *(John Sinclair)*

AEC Reliance 7431SP (FAC11), on the left, and MWG367 (FPD152) a Leyland Tiger Cub, both wear Fife's coach livery when seen at Cupar bus depot in August 1963. They have both been bodied by Alexander in the plain, yet stylish, type of body work of the late-1950s and early-1960s. *(John Sinclair)*

OMS270 (FPD194), a Tiger Cub seen here in the mid-1970s at St Andrews bus station and garage, was new to Walter Alexander as PD194 but shortly thereafter transferred to the Alexander (Fife) subsidiary. This was an Anstruther-based bus and is on a one-man operated service; hence the 'pay as you enter' hinged board on the front nearside. A sturdy Fifer in a business-like cap occupies the seat behind the driver. An Alexander-bodied Y-type Leyland Leopard can be glimpsed in the shed behind. *(Dr George Fairbairn)*

Alexander-bodied Royal Tiger EMS168 (FPC50) of St Andrews depot was used extensively between the Fife town and Glasgow, where it is seen here at rest. Operated jointly with Alexander (Midland), service 100 was a Saturday-only service and only saw two journeys in each direction, one bus from both companies. The journey was a hefty 2 hours 50 minutes in each direction. *(John Sinclair)*

Two Tiger Cubs from St Andrews depot are seen in the bus station in Dundee awaiting their departure times for their journeys back across the Tay Bridge in October 1969. The boot areas between the two Fife buses and their Northern counterpart, all carry subtle differences around the rear. The Fife vehicles are MWG371 (FPD156) and OMS254 (FPD178). *(John Sinclair)*

This was one of two Leyland Royal Tigers that were rebuilt as one-man operated buses in the mid-1960s. They received completely new front ends with this vehicle also receiving new windows too. A complete transformation from the way it used to look as seen by a similar type of bus earlier on in these pages. This one belonged to Cupar depot and is seen at rest in the main shed area. *(John Sinclair)*

Leyland Tiger PS1, BWG510 (FPA105) takes a well-earned break on the harbour wall in its home town of Anstruther. It is on the service 361 which was a local service running between Anstruther Harbour and St Andrews via Dunino. It was an infrequent service and only took about half-an-hour each way. *(Andy Wood)*

A dreary, wet day in St Andrews sees Leyland Tiger Cub OMS262 (FPD186), sitting awaiting its time to move on stance, to depart on its homeward journey back to Anstruther Harbour. This run was operated by the driver only as the sign displays a notice to pay the driver on entry. These signs would not be shown had a conductor been on board. *(Brian McDevitt)*

Alexander-bodied Leyland Tiger Cub KMS474 (FPD105), of Cupar depot, is seen sitting in Tay Street, Perth, by the river's edge. This bus is wearing the original coach livery of cream with Ayres red relief band and a red roof. All the roofs on the coach liveried vehicles were eventually all repainted cream as they were called into the workshops for their routine maintenance. It was withdrawn and sold to Muir's in Kirkcaldy in 1975.

DWG525 (FPC29) is a Leyland Royal Tiger with bodywork by Leyland themselves. It is a 1952 vehicle with dual-purpose seating and manages to catch the sun broadside before an early evening return to its home depot of Cupar. This vehicle was withdrawn and sold on to a dealership in Preston in 1970. *(Robert Dickson Collection)*

RMS723 (FPD234) was in the first batch of buses ordered by Alexander (Fife) after the split in 1961. It was also the last of the Leyland Tiger Cubs ordered by the Fife Company. FPD234 was a Cupar-allocated vehicle and is seen here in Glasgow on the Saturday-only service from St Andrews to Glasgow and back. There were only two runs in each direction simultaneously leaving St Andrews and Glasgow at 1000 and 1400. The service was shared with Alexander (Midland). This must be the 1400 return from Glasgow and would take almost three hours to return to the Fife coast. *(John Sinclair)*

Alexander-bodied Leyland Tiger Cubs MWG371 (FPD156), OMS252 (FPD176), OMS254 (FPD178) and Leyland Royal Tiger DWG691 (FPC34) line up and make a fine looking display at St Andrews depot. FPC34 was scrapped by Alexander's in 1970, while the others all vanquished at Muir's, Kirkcaldy, in the mid-1970s. *(John Sinclair)*

Alexander-bodied AEC Reliance BXA426B (FAC30), has just arrived in St Andrews on a miserable looking day about 1970. I don't know the exact date, but I am using conjecture due to the fact that the coach still has a red roof as originally applied and the type of car on view. I hope the lady with the rain hat and suit cases hasn't just arrived on holiday! *(Brian McDevitt)*

It is some time in the mid-1960s and we find Alexander-bodied Guy Arab LUF, GMS412 (FGA2) parked up in Glasgow displaying window stickers showing 'St Andrews' and 'Duplicate'. I can only surmise that this would have been a duplicate bus on the summer-only Saturday service 100 between St Andrews and Glasgow. There were only two buses in each direction on Saturdays only during June, July and August each year. I would imagine that the extra bus would be needed on more than one occasion as the Fife coast was a popular holiday spot for Glaswegians. *(Len Wright)*

Leyland Tiger Cub MWG378 (FPD163), with Alexander bodywork, is employed here on a typical service that was suitable for the type of vehicle. The service 301 was the St Andrews circular town service and basically ran hourly around the town all day. This was a one-man operated service, which must have been quite boring when you consider it would go one way around town, then back the opposite way. This is all it did all day. *(Brian McDevitt)*

Two classic looking, and contrasting body styles, by the coach-building side of the Alexander bus empire are seen here in the form of AEC Reliance's BXA424B (FAC28), and 7431 (FAC11). The Y-type was considered to be modern and 'American' looking, when it was first introduced with its slanted panoramic windows. By contrast, the earlier body styling was also pleasant looking with its clean lines, and bright inside due to the extra windows on the curved roof sides. FAC11 wears an apt side advert for Haig Whisky proclaiming to be the 'Discerning golfers' handy cap'. *(John Sinclair)*

The date is September 1964 and we find Alexander-bodied Leyland Tiger Cub MWG367 (FPD152) showing a good example of the high cleaning standards from Cupar depot. It is showing that it had been used on the service 340 which was a Monday to Saturday service between Cupar and Kirkcaldy Esplanade. There were only four runs in each direction between the two and ran via Kingskettle, Markinch and Thornton. FPD152 was withdrawn in 1975 and ended up like so many others at Muir's in Kirkcaldy. *(John Sinclair)*

Daimler Fleetline PXA635J (FRF35) catches the sun as it passes the ruins of St Andrews Cathedral in 1974. Apart from being the home of golf, St Andrews is a beautiful town with a famous university. It also has its own little depot which that year, housed a good selection of AEC Reliances and Tiger Cubs. *(Dr George Fairbairn)*

PXA635J (FRF35) of St Andrews depot makes an unscheduled photographic stop as it makes its way down the coast towards Leven, the southernmost end of the route from Dundee. Perhaps this run is terminating in St Andrews itself as there is a sticker in the lower nearside window displaying the name of the coastal town.

A strong Cupar connection here in the summer of 1974, as FRD151 on the left has obviously been on a run to the county town recently, while Albion Viking DXA407C (FNV7) is a vehicle belonging to Cupar depot. Perhaps it is on a long layover or just parked up 'out the way' to make space on the forecourt area. *(John Sinclair)*

DXA412C (FNV12) waits at St Andrews depot before its next run which is a part route run to Leuchars railway station. The 355 service had many 'part route' runs incorporated within the timetable as it was almost two hours and twenty minutes for the run between Leven and Dundee. This run must have been one-man operated as it is displaying a 'pay as you enter' notice on the lower nearside windscreen. *(Dr George Fairbairn)*

Alexander-bodied AEC Reliance BXA432B (FAC36), looks like it is being made ready to go out on a private hire. This Anstruther-based vehicle is seen in an off-road parking area, just outside the entrance to its home depot on Pittenweem Road to the south of the town. *(Brian McDevitt)*

Alexander-bodied Albion Viking NXA648H (FNV48) is seen sitting outside the main entrance to the depot on Pittenweem Road in Anstruther. It will be used on one of the infrequent runs on the service 361 to St Andrews just up the coast. There were four runs to St Andrews on a Monday to Saturday with six runs returning. There was also one late run from St Andrews on a Sunday night. *(Roger Norton)*

Anstruther-allocated Albion Viking HXA43E (FNV34), has just arrived in St Andrews and dropped its small consignment of passengers off while on the service 355 from Leven. It would be about another fifty minutes before the bus reached its destination from here.

Leyland Leopard XXA859M (FPE59) is seen within the confines at Cupar depot shortly before the depot closed its doors for the last time in 1981. Even at this stage, Cupar was still presenting well maintained and clean buses. Service 66 was a service from Cupar to the new town of Glenrothes which took just over an hour and travelled via Springfield, Auchtermuchty and Falkland. *(John Sinclair)*

Albion Viking DXA402C (FNV2) leaves Perth Bus Station at the start of a journey that will take just under two hours to complete. Service 336 travelled via Newburgh and took in many stopping places on the route through central north Fife.

Sitting in the shed at St Andrews is PXA635J (FRF35), waiting its next turn of duty for the day. Typical of the ECW Bodywork is the white/cream window rubbers which suited these vehicles. This view also shows how compact the depot looks within its limited confines. *(John Law)*

Cupar depot always seemed to turn out well presented vehicles as exemplified by Albion Vikings FXA721D (FNV21) and FXA724D (FNV24). Even shortly before the depots closure in 1981, when the company was a part of the corporate Scottish Bus Group, they were still taking pride in their buses. *(John Sinclair)*

DXA410C (FNV10), was a St Andrews allocated Albion Viking seen here taking a rest in Dundee Seagate bus station having earlier arrived on a service 305, which was a local service between Tayport and Dundee. This was another of the services that operated in the northern part of Fife that was one-man operated.

New in 1963, AEC Reliance AXA224A (FAC24) is seen sitting in its home yard at Anstruther bus depot during the early 1970s. These earlier Y-type bodies had a slightly different look to the destination display area where the Destination and the route number appear to look separate. Later bodies just had the single aperture displaying both destination and route number. *(Robert Dickson)*

AEC Reliance BXA433B (FAC37), was one of St Andrews' own allocation of buses, and is here being used on the long-haul service 355 from Dundee. The driver will barely have time to catch his breath before heading another hour-and-a-half down the coast towards Leven bus station.

Anstruther depot is displaying the type of power that was typical of the type of vehicles used in the northeast area of Fife. Two AEC Reliance vehicles, AXA225A (FAC25) and BXA424B (FAC28) stand alongside Albion Viking FXA713D (FNV13) in a display of power. It should be noted that FAC25, on the left, has a single-leaf coach door as opposed to the twin-leaf folding door as used on the other vehicles on view. *(Roger Norton)*

The journey to Dundee on the service 353 would be a piece of cake for Cupar-allocated Leyland Leopard, OXA462H (FPE12). It is seen to be a well patronised service as it prepares to leave Cupar Crossgate on the second leg of its journey to the 'City of Discovery' on the bi-hourly service. *(Brian McDevitt)*

Dundee Seagate bus station is the location here as we see a study of a couple of rear ends. Eastern Coach Works bodied Fleetline PXA640J (FRF40) sits beside Y-type Leopard XXA859M (FPE59) as they wait to depart on various services back to Fife in July 1975. The bustle area of the Fleetline was the same for all body types, regardless of manufacturer, while the under-floor-engined Leopard enjoyed a generous boot space at the rear. Alexander's used the rear dome of the Y-type body and used it as the front dome for their Daimler Fleetline bodies. *(John Sinclair)*

At first glance we see three similar coaches parked up inside Cupar depot in about 1972. What we have is actually three different types of vehicle chassis with the same Alexander Y-type bodies. On the left is 1970 Leyland Leopard OXA462H (FPE12), whilst in the centre we have 1969 Albion Viking NXA647H (FNV47). Last, but by no means least, on the right is 1966 AEC Reliance GXA157D (FAC57). Variety is the spice of life indeed. *(John Sinclair)*

Alexander-bodied AEC Reliance BXA431B (FAC35), an Anstruther-based vehicle, is being used on the one-man operated service 301, which was the St Andrews circular town service. A journey around town on this service was only fourteen minutes, and I believe may have been done by vehicles in between turns on the 361 service from Anstruther when photographed in September 1970. *(John Sinclair)*

Anstruther was home to several Alexander-bodied AECs, another of which is BXA427B (FAC31). It is pictured in the depot yard on 10 August 1978, and would be used later on that day on the local 361 service to St Andrews, which only took half an hour. It is seen wearing the original coach livery with the red roof, although these were later repainted cream. Note the absence of emergency exit at the rear of this coach as this was the norm when built in 1964. *(Robert Dickson)*

PXA635J (FRF35) was seen in an earlier image on the same service and carrying the same window sticker on the lower nearside front window. At least in this image the bus looks a good bit more patronised than it did in the earlier photograph. These ECW-bodied Daimler Fleetlines were quite distinguished looking with their white window rubbers. *(Brian McDevitt)*

Leyland Leopards were not as common as the AEC Reliance in these parts, but here WXA950M (FPE50) makes a welcoming change. As in keeping with a lot of the photographs, the reader will have noticed that the predominating service in these parts was the 355. FPE50 is on this service when photographed having arrived in the town in a short, part route working from Dundee on a dreary looking day during July 1974. *(John Sinclair)*

SXA63K (FRF63) was one of seven Alexander-bodied Daimler Fleetline buses to arrive in Fife in 1971, and was allocated to Cupar depot from where it is seen exiting. That year, there was also a delivery of five Fleetlines with bodywork by Northern Counties that were transferred to Alexander (Midland) after only four years' service. (John Sinclair)

The AEC Reliance was a well suited vehicle for use on the routes around the north-east parts of Fife. Five are lined up in Anstruther depot in the latter half of the 1970s. They are, from left to right, BXA441B (FAC45), GXA155D (FAC55), 7421SP (FAC1), BXA424B (FAC28) and AXA224A (FAC24) (Brian McDevitt)

A solitary Bristol RELL, JXA931F (FE31), cuts a lonely figure sitting amid the more familiar AEC Reliance-type vehicle found in Anstruther depot in the mid 1970s. The sharp-eyed reader will have noticed the predominance of the 355 route number on vehicles based at Anstruther. *(Roger Norton)*

Another of Anstruther's AEC buses, BXA432B (FAC36) has obviously been used on the service 361 from St. Andrews, with perhaps a run around St Andrews town centre on the circular service 301. This is when the 'Pay as You Enter' board would have been displayed as that service was one-man operated. *(Robert Dickson)*

BXA433B (FAC37) was an AEC Reliance with bus windows, and is seen here having just arrived on a short, part route working, from Dundee on the popular service 355. The bus company operated a special timetable for this service during the summer months, when many holidaymakers arrived in the town. *(John Sinclair)*

As pointed out earlier, the service 305 was a local affair running between Tayport and Dundee. It was also pointed out that it was a one-man operated service. This is clearly displayed by the 'Pay as You Enter' board on show in the nearside of the windscreen. AEC Reliance BXA434B (FAC38) is the shift vehicle on this day in September 1970 and is parked up in the layover area beside CWG53 (NRB75), a Leyland Titan in the fleet of Alexander (Northern). *(John Sinclair)*

Alexander-bodied AEC Reliance BXA433B (FAC37), was one of the more regular performers at St Andrews depot. It would seem that it was regularly the shift bus on service 355, as seen here, shortly after arriving on a part route working from Dundee on a rather overcast day in June 1978. There is a typical advert for Haig Scotch Whisky adorning the side panel of the bus. *(John Sinclair)*

An AEC Reliance, probably from St Andrews depot as they had an abundance of them, seems to have lost its front grille as it is seen having just arrived on the arduous 355 service from Leven to Dundee. BXA433B (FAC37) looks like it is on a quiet run as there are no passengers on board. *(Brian McDevitt)*

Albion Viking HXA35E (FNV35) with Alexander Y-type bodywork is seen being readied for its next turn of duty for the day, no doubt being on some mundane local working around the town. It was only a year old when photographed here in 1968, and is seen displaying one of the many adverts for Haig Whisky that adorned most of the buses in the fleet around that time. *(John Sinclair)*

WXA950M (FPE50) was one of the 1974 intake of Leopards, as usual bodied by Walter Alexander at their plant in Falkirk. Even when wearing coach livery, it is still very much noticeable how clean the buses were kept under Alexander's control. This bus is pictured in Cupar, heading homeward to St Andrews on the bi-hourly service 364 from Perth. *(John Sinclair)*

One of the Albion Vikings allocated to St Andrews depot DXA411C (FNV11), is seen at the entrance to the Kinkell Braes Caravan Park at the southern end of the town in the early 1970s. The service number is 401, but I cannot trace if this was a true number for the run depicted, although the bus has a destination board with 'Kinkell' in the window. Perhaps it was a summertime-only special service. *(John Sinclair)*

The evoluion of the body style used by Walter Alexander can be clearly seen in this image taken at Anstruther depot around the early part of 1970. Leyland Tiger PS1 BWG510 (FPA105) on the left, has the older body style from 1948, whilst the two 1960 built, Leyland Tiger cubs in the middle, OMS255 and OMS270 (FPD179 and FPD194) carry the 'intermediate', yet stylish, bodywork. The AEC Reliance on the right, GXA154D (FAC54) has the famous Y-type of body style that was well known throughout the country. *(John Sinclair)*

A mid-1970s image of AEC Reliance BXA441B (FAC45) sitting in the yard at its home depot in Anstruther. This vehicle carries a side advert for Haig Whisky. It might be fun to try and find out how many different styles of Haig adverts can be seen on Fife's buses in these pages. *(Robert Dickson)*

Cupar depot is once again the location as we find AEC Reliance BXA423B (FAC27) and Leyland Leopard XXA861M (FPE61) gleaming in the bright sun during a mid-1970s visit. The AEC Reliance had been used on the service 366 which ran from the town to Ladybank via Springfield and Bow of Fife. *(John Sinclair)*

The location on this summer's day in about 1972 is Glasgow Buchanan Street. AEC Reliance BXA433B (FAC37) had arrived with the service 100 which was a Saturday-only service departing from St Andrews at 1000. This service arrived in Glasgow at 1250 and headed back to the Fife town at 1400 on a journey of similar length. There was a service run by Alexander (Midland) which left Glasgow at 1000 and headed towards Fife and back using the same timings. This service ran during June, July and August only and served those using the Fife town which was a popular destination with holidaying Glaswegians. *(John Sinclair)*

Service number 10. Yes, this is a bus service! The Royal Mail has operated post bus services in the more extreme rural areas, not only in Fife, but throughout the country. BSF96L, a Commer 2000LB with Rootes eleven-seat bodywork, is spotted in Cupar waiting to depart for Peat Inn during 1973. There was a morning route and an afternoon route, each with slight variations too numerous to mention here. *(Barry Sanjana)*

A wee look at some of the buses operated by Williamson of Gauldry before they became part of Moffat & Williamson starting with TUH361. It was an AEC Bridgemaster chassis with Park Royal bodywork. New to Cardiff Corporation as their 361 in 1960, it then passed to Newton's of Dingwall before arriving here. This was dated April 1973. *(Barry Sanjana)*

196JVK was a Leyland Atlantean with early Alexander bodywork for this type of chassis. It was new in 1961 to Tyneside PTE and operated as their 196. It stayed with them until being acquired by Williamsons in September 1972. *(Barry Sanjana)*

VTX428 was an AEC Regent V with Weymann bodywork. It was new in 1958 to Rhondda in Wales as their 428, but was acquired in August 1971 from the renamed Western Welsh. Like Rennies of Dunfermline, these buses would primarily be used on school contract runs. *(Barry Sanjana)*

VFG535L was a Ford R1014 with bodywork by Duple. This one was new to Williamsons in January 1973, and is barely three months old when photographed in their yard in Gauldry. *(Barry Sanjana)*

EHD452 was another AEC Regent V chassis, but this one had bodywork by Metro-Cammell. This vehicle was new in 1960 to Yorkshire Woollen, and it was from them that Williamsons acquired the vehicle in August 1971. *(Barry Sanjana)*

LJX198 was the third AEC Regent V chassis owned by Williamsons. This one also carried a Weymann body and was new in 1959 to Hebble of Halifax. Once again, Williamsons were only the second owners of the vehicle when purchased from Hebble in December 1970. *(Barry Sanjana)*

EWS844D is seen with Moffat & Williamson in spring 1981, three years after merging with Moffat of Cardenden. It was, by this time, fifteen years old, having been new in 1966 to Edinburgh Corporation Transport. It is seen wearing the blue and white colours of Williamsons. *(John Law)*

EGS914 belonged to T. D. Niven, an independent operator from St Andrews that was bought by Alexander (Fife) in 1967. This Leyland TD7 with McLennan bodywork never made it into the Fife fleet and is seen languishing at the rear of her former yard. It is presumed this vehicle was scrapped. *(Peter Relf Collection)*

KSC738 was another vehicle operating in the fleet of Nivens. It was a Daimler CVD6 chassis with Plaxton bodywork when re-registered in 1953. It originally had a body by the Yorkshire Yacht Company when new in 1948. Again, this vehicle also never made the Fife fleet, and it is not known what became of it after 1967. *(Peter Relf Collection)*

St Andrews-based AEC Reliance GXA146D (FAC46) takes a well-earned rest after its journey to Dundee in the early part of the 1980s. Although fitted with coach seats, this vehicle has been repainted into bus livery, a practice that happened often when vehicles were nearing the end of their lives with the company.

Leyland Leopard XSG68R (FPE68) and Daimler Fleetline VRS147L (FRF78), both with Alexander bodies, are pictured parked up at their home depot at Newburgh, a depot that was often exposed to the elements thanks to its proximity to the River Tay, which was to the rear of the vehicles. *(Brian McDevitt)*

WXA946M (FPE46), a Newburgh-based Leyland Leopard with Alexander Y-type coach body, is almost at Perth's bus station as it rounds the curve at the entrance to the railway station. Service 37 originated in Kirkcaldy, and reached the Fair City, by way of Strathmiglo, in just under two hours. *(Paul Redmond)*

Mk1 Ailsa LSX40P (FRA40) sits at the head of a long line of other Ailsas, with the odd Daimler Fleetline thrown in for good measure. The location is of course, Leuchars railway station, the terminus, and starting point for those travelling to or from any major golfing event held at the famous old course in St Andrews. At one time the crowds would have managed to get the train direct to St Andrews before the line closed in the mid-1960s. *(Andrew Cook)*

Daimler Fleetline RXA50J (FRF50) has just left Cupar Crossgate on the service 65 to Newburgh on a miserable summer's day in June 1983. This service was one of those infrequent services that Fife operated from time to time. It was advertised on the timetables as a service between Cupar and Perth, but in reality, only one journey each way, per day operated. All other services ran between the county town and Newburgh. *(Brian McDevitt)*

The Alexander Y-type body was well suited to most chassis types available at the time. This is epitomised by two Fords in the shape of HSF559N (FT14) and HSF557N (FT12), as well as Leopard XXA861M (FPE61) and AEC Reliance GXA157D (FAC57). All are seen sitting in their home depot at Cupar in April 1981. *(Richard Huggins)*

A good idea of the location of Newburgh depot in its proximity to the River Tay can be seen in this image of Daimler Fleetline NXA633H (FRF33), and Leyland Leopard XXA859M (FPE59) taken in May 1984. The Fleetline is seen to be displaying a 'C' depot suffix letter; this is probably due to the vehicle being recently re-allocated from Cowdenbeath. One early evening run on the service 23 did terminate at Gateside on a part route run from Cupar. I would imagine this would be to accommodate a workers run. *(Richard Huggins)*

Y-type Leopard YSF82S (FPE82) wears a wrap-around advert for C&V Furnishings Ltd, a local retailer based in Methil, when photographed in April 1981. Service 94 was a local, infrequent service between St Andrews and Balmullo, a village about five or six miles to the north-west of St Andrews, and had a journey time of less than half-an-hour. *(Richard Huggins)*

B207FFS (FLT7) was one of five Leyland Tigers bought by Fife Scottish in 1985 with Alexander 'TC' type body work. They were primarily used on long-distance express runs from the Kingdom to Glasgow but, on occasion, could be found doing more mundane work such as this run on the service 97 from Leven to St Andrews via Largoward in May 1985. *(Richard Huggins)*

Leyland Leopard WXA946M (FPE46) sits outside the main shed doors at its home depot at Newburgh in 1981, having just arrived on one of the many short workings from Perth that terminate in the Fife outpost. *(Richard Huggins)*

Daimler Fleetline PXA639J (FRF39) with bodywork by Eastern Coach Works is found sitting in a car park in Cupar, along with a couple of Alexander-bodied buses belonging to Moffat & Williamson. These buses parked up in here waiting for the afternoon journeys from the town's Bell Baxter High School. *(Clive A. Brown)*

St Catherine Street in Cupar is the location as we find Leopard WFS153W (FPE153) newly arrived on the service 53 from Dundee. It had a journey time of just over forty minutes with only seven journeys in each direction during the week, half that again on a Saturday. The location hasn't changed much and looks pretty similar today as it did in 1983 when this photograph was taken. *(Brian McDevitt)*

Alexander Y-type Leyland Leopard PSX188Y (FPE188) is seen uplifting a couple of passengers in Victoria Street, Ladybank. This is an interchange bus stop as it sits adjacent to the town's railway station. Service 66 was a Glenrothes to Cupar run which travelled via Falkland, Auchtermuchty and Springfield. *(Brian McDevitt)*

Leyland Atlantean NRG157M (FRN7) with Alexander H45/29F AL-type of bodywork, is seen here parked up at the bus depot at Newburgh, but with a Cowdenbeath shed allocation suffix letter. Ten Leyland Atlanteans arrived in Fife in 1985 from Grampian Regional Transport with dual doors. They were quickly changed to a single-door layout which increased the seating capacity by seven, giving an H45/36F layout. *(Clive A. Brown)*

The SMS P batch of Fleetlines were far travelled. It was new to Alexander (Midland) before moving on to various other owners including Kelvin, Western, Northern and Highland. SMS129P (729) is seen in the beautiful setting of St Andrews wearing the large logo livery as applied to vehicles around 1987. *(Gordon Stirling)*

Y-type Leyland Leopard YSF78S (FPE78) makes headway down Scott Street in Perth, as it makes a return journey back to Newburgh on one of the short part-route workings. The journey time was just over the half-hour and would take in Bridge of Earn, Baiglie Inn and Abernethy. *(Malcolm Audsley)*

CSF167W (267) is sporting a bit of repair work, as a new front off-side panel has just had an undercoat applied. The front panel itself still has a bit of paintwork needed. This Y-type Leopard had dual purpose seating and was ideal for either local or, as in this instance, long-distance work. 267 would have made the journey from St Andrews which was almost two hours driving. When this photo was taken in the late 1980s, it was hard to imagine that only a few years previously, the bus would have travelled all the way to Glasgow on a journey close to four hours long. *(Clive A. Brown)*

XXA373M (FRF73) was Fife's last new Daimler Fleetline, entering service in 1973, the same year it was exhibited at the Scottish Motor Show. Allocated to Newburgh, it is shown while operating a part route working on the service 23 and its terminal point will be Strathmiglo. It is my humble opinion that these handsome looking vehicles suited the 'Large Logo' livery.

Ailsa Mk1 LSX17P (817) must have evoked a few memories when seen leaving St Andrews bus station in the late 1980s with a service 95 for Dundee. The 'A' depot code was at one time used to denote vehicles allocated to Anstruther depot, but after Anstruther depot closed in 1981, the 'A' letter was used by Leven's Aberhill depot which had previously used 'AL'. *(Malcolm Audsley)*

Mk2 Leyland National YSX928W (328) is being used on the mundane service 9 around St Andrews town centre on the circular service. The red paintwork on the lower side panel is looking rather the worse for wear, as it would appear to have been applied without the usual pink undercoat. *(Malcolm Audsley)*

Newburgh depot is the allocated depot for Leyland Leopard PSX189Y (FPE189). This was one of the last batch of Y-type Leopards delivered new to Fife Scottish in 1982, and was numerically Fife's last new Y-type. It is currently owned by a small group of Fife drivers with the author having the main share. This batch was also unique in being delivered with no overhead luggage racks. *(Clive A. Brown)*

In the days when this photograph was taken, (about 1989), there were only three runs each way between St Andrews and Edinburgh. CFS110S (210) is seen getting ready to pull into the stance in St Andrews on one of those runs carrying 'Cityliner' branding on the front panel. *(Gary Seamarks)*

1989 sees another of Fife's Mk1 Ailsas, LSX14P (814), sitting outside the depot in St Andrews. I am unsure if it may have worked on one of the services between Leven and St Andrews, or if it had been re-allocated there, but still retaining the Aberhill shed code. (By this time the 'A' shed code was used for Aberhill, as Anstruther had closed eight years previous to this). *(Malcolm Audsley)*

Leyland National Mk2, YSX933W (333), makes its way down South Street in St Andrews with the finials of the Holy Trinity Church in the background. This is about 1989, just a year or so before the bus received the new style of fleet name as seen on page 74 in the *Fife Buses* book. *(Malcolm Audsley)*

D521DSX (421) is a Leyland Tiger with Alexander P-type bodywork. The rather square style of this type of body styling earned these buses the unfortunate nickname of 'Portacabins'. 421 drops two or three passengers off, having just arrived in St Andrews on one of the short workings from Dundee. *(Malcolm Audsley)*

Y-type Leopard WFS140W (140) has arrived back in its home territory in St Andrews from either Perth or Cupar Crossgate on a service 64. This was about the middle to late-1980s, a time when the large Fife Scottish corporate fleet name was quite prominent, and dominant, on vehicles. *(Malcolm Audsley)*

Y-type Leopard YSF93S (93), is seen on its way to the bus station in St Andrews, having just completed a short working on the 95 service from Dundee. Perhaps because of the location and the beautiful day, the bus seems to be patronised by a few elderly passengers. *(Gordon Stirling)*

Not too long out of Stirling, and we find Leyland Leopard CSF169W (269) making steady progress through the Hillfoots in Clackmannanshire on the road back to St Andrews. 269 had dual purpose seating making it ideal for use on a service such as the 23. The large logo livery suited the styling of the Alexander Y-type of bodywork. *(Robert Dickson)*

SMS130P (730) was one of a batch of former Alexander (Midland) Fleetlines that found their way into the Fife Fleet via Northern and Highland bus companies. It is seen in Dundee heading back towards the Kingdom, and Cupar in particular in March 1988, a time when rear-engined double-deckers were rare in the Fife Fleet. *(Gary Seamarks)*

Duple Dominant Mk1-bodied Leyland Leopard GSG133T (FPE133), of St Andrews depot, has obviously been used on a private hire as it sits in the layover area at Perth bus station. Fife ordered thirty Duple Dominants in 1978 and they were of a mixture of both versions, in no particular type order. The Mk1 Dominants had a shallow windscreen compared to the Mk2 version. *(Malcolm Audsley)*

St Andrews has always been a favourite destination for both holidaymakers and day-trippers. This is seen to be the case as Midland Scottish, Alexander bodied Seddon, 365UMY (MSE1), a vehicle specially converted for the use of wheelchair users, is making ready to depart back to the Alloa area from St Andrews bus park. *(Malcolm Audsley)*

Daimler Fleetline VRS147L (FRF78) has just entered Dundee bus station with window stickers displaying 'Wormit' and 'Newport'. This is a mystery to me as that would place it on a run operated by Northern Scottish between Dundee and Gauldry. This is one of three vehicles with Alexander bodywork acquired from Grampian Buses in 1983 with dual doors. It would be converted to single-door soon after acquisition.

St Andrews always turned out immaculate looking buses, YSX933W (333) being no exception. It is seen sometime about 1990 on a beautiful late spring day on local service 10 to Bogward via Canongate. This appears to be a well-patronised bus as it is seen leaving the town's bus station with shoppers heading home after a pleasant day's shopping. *(Gordon Stirling)*

C806USG (906) passes between the RNLI Lifeboat Station, seen on the right of the photograph, and the Fisheries Museum which is off to the left of the vehicle, as it makes steady progress passing along Anstruther High Street. This is also the harbour area near a certain famous, renowned chip shop. *(Patrick Castelli)*

Alexander-bodied Mercedes Benz minibus K489FFS (89) makes progress on its rural service 61 to St Monans, a small holiday town two three miles to the south-west of Anstruther. These small minibuses were ideally suited to the rural nature of many of the services in the east Neuk. *(Ewan Wood)*

The driver of VLT77 (77), a Reeve Burgess-bodied Mercedes minibus, looks bored as he awaits his departure time on a local service 1, the 'Scooniehill Circular', within St Andrews in July 1998. This particular location in South Street has always been a favourite with bus enthusiasts taking photographs. *(Malcolm Audsley)*

Another minibus being used on another of the local service around St Andrews. Alexander-bodied Mercedes Benz K488FFS (88), is being deployed on service S2, the 'Tom Morris Drive Circular'. It is just another of the routes in the town to benefit from the use of minibuses. *(Malcolm Audsley)*

I must admit to having little experience with the Leyland Titans that Stagecoach brought up from Selkent to Fife in the later part of the 1990s. I believe they were a temporary stop gap arrangement between the Volvo Citybus clearout, and the Volvo Olympians that Stagecoach eventually flooded Fife with. Seen leaving Dundee bus station with a short working for Tayport, this bus may have been allocated to the outstation at Newport. A66THX (766) was an 'all-Leyland' vehicle and was new to London Regional Transport in 1984. *(Malcolm Audsley)*

G337KKW (737) was one of two Alexander RL-type-bodied Leyland Olympians brought to Fife in 1992 from East Midland Buses. This one is seen here being used on a limited stop service X59 from St Andrews to Edinburgh due to the vehicle being fitted with dual-purpose seating. *(Ewan Wood)*

The small bridge on Drummochy Road, Lower Largo, is the location here as we find Alexander-bodied Volvo Citybus C795USG (915) making steady progress on the run from St Andrews to Edinburgh by way of the Fife coast. The Crusoe Hotel is a well-known local establishment. *(Ewan Wood)*

Minibuses could even be used on school services in this area, as witnessed here by the presence of another of the many Alexander-bodied Mercedes buses allocated at the time to St Andrews. K491FFS (91), despite showing 'Waid Academy' on the destination blind, would in fact, be taking these pupils home from school at the end of the school day. *(Ewan Wood)*

Plaxton Premier-bodied B10M, L586HSG (586), is sitting at the departure point at Shore Street in Anstruther before departing on the arduous journey to Glasgow. I can't remember there being an X28 to Glasgow, but I do remember it being the X26 and X27. These two services only had slight route variations between Dunfermline and Kirkcaldy when I was doing express work. *(Ewan Wood)*

Moffat & Williamson's Alexander-bodied Leyland Atlantean UGG390R is seen on one of their local services that ran around St Andrews in the early 1990s. This bus was new to Greater Glasgow PTE in June 1977 and served as their fleet number LA1171. *(Gordon Stirling)*

September 1993 is the date when we see TPJ67S, a Bristol LH with ECW bodywork. It was new in 1977 to 'London Country' but was purchased by Moffat & Williamson in January 1991 from Eastbourne Borough Transport. They sold it on, in November 1994 to MacEwan of Amisfield. *(Malcolm Audsley)*

1993 is once more the date as GMS299S, a former Midland Scottish Leyland Leopard, and LFJ850W, a Bristol LH with ECW body work are both found enjoying the sun inside the Moffat & Williamson depot at St Fort. *(Malcolm Audsley)*

St Fort depot is once again the location as we find D142RAK and D114OWG, two Dodge minibuses with Reeve Burgess bodywork. They were both new to South Yorkshire Transport in 1987 but were with the Fife independent six years later. *(Malcolm Audsley)*

D971TKC was another Dodge Minibus, but this one had bodywork by Northern Counties. This vehicle, also new in 1987, came from its original owner, Merseyside Transport, after six years. *(Malcolm Audsley)*

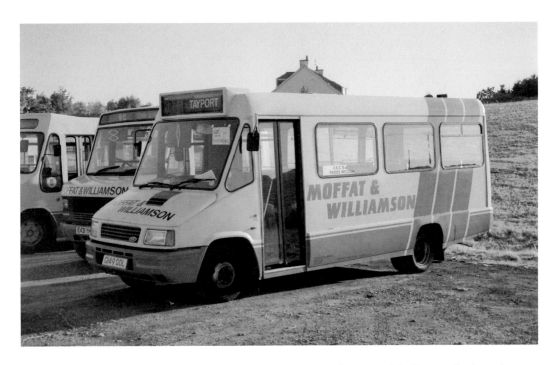

Once again at St Fort depot in 1993, G149GOL, a Ford Iveco with Caetano bodywork, sits awaiting its next turn of duty, no doubt on one of the local services that Moffat & Williamson provide in the north of the county. This vehicle was sold on a year or two later to Choice Travel of Wolverhampton. *(Malcolm Audsley)*

Renault E186UWF and Mercedes Benz E431YHL, both bodied by Reeve Burgess, are also found in St Fort depot on a rare bright day in August 1993. As can be seen by the destination blinds, these vehicles were extensively used on the various town and local routes throughout the area. *(Malcolm Audsley)*

Leyland Tiger BSK790 with Plaxton Paramount bodywork, like the previous photographs, is found in the sun at St Fort in August 1993. It was one of the coaches belonging to Moffat & Williamson at the time, and often seen out on tour or on hires. The registration number is still used by the company to this day on their coaches. *(Malcolm Audsley)*

Another of the former Leyland Leopards originally new to Alexander (Midland) in 1978 was GMS280S. Moffat & Williamson removed the stepped aluminium waistband and added a black plastic strip lower down the body. Considered to be an improvement to some, but not to others. *(Malcolm Audsley)*

Back on the streets of St Andrews, Iveco G315TKO is busy plying its trade on a local town service route in July 1993. The building in the background is the ruin of Blackfriars Chapel, to be found on South Street in the town centre. *(Malcolm Audsley)*

Alexander-bodied Daimler Fleetline PRG123J, new in February 1971 to Aberdeen Corporation, and WTN658H, an Alexander-bodied Leyland Atlantean, new in 1970 to Tyne & Wear PTE are seen parked up in Cupar on a driecht day in June 1983. WTN658H was a much travelled vehicle and was originally dual doored. It was converted to single-door use when briefly with Moffat & Williamson in the 1980s. *(Brian McDevitt)*

New to Moffat & Williamson in January 2000, V117ESL is seen here in St Andrews town centre employed on local service work. It is a Mercedes Benz minibus with Plaxton Beaver 2 bodywork. *(Suzy Scott)*

A surprise purchase by Stagecoach in 1992 from Ribble, TMS405X (205) was a former vehicle in the fleet of Alexander (Midland). This Y-type-bodied Leyland Leopard is seen in South Street, St Andrews, employed on service 9, a local circular service around the town. *(Ewan Wood)*

One of the Alexander-bodied Ailsa Mk1s allocated to St Andrews was LSX32P (832). It is loading a small handful of passengers before it heads off on the long-established service 95 to Dundee. A typical area of these vehicles that suffered damage from overhanging branches, the peaked dome shows the red area where the fibreglass has had repair work carried out.

The Alexander-bodied Mercedes Minibus was first introduced in 1993 and was a great asset when used in sparsely populated areas as it suited the needs of the type of services they were deployed on. K487FFS (87) is used on such a working when seen in St Andrews on local service S3 on a bitter winter's day about 1993. The driving snow had only just stopped as witnessed by the radiator grille. *(Ewan Wood)*

E910KSG (909) was one a duo of Volvo B10s with Alexander RV bodywork in the Fife fleet. They were transferred from a Western Scottish order in 1987 and seated seventy passengers in relative comfort. 909 seen in Anstruther having just arrived at Shore Street outside the public library. Some services used to terminate on Toll Road near the holiday and caravan park. *(Ewan Wood)*

Cupar Crossgate is the setting for L584HSG (584) as it picks its passengers up, perhaps heading to Edinburgh for a day's shopping. By now, the Plaxton-bodied B10M coach was the standard coach used on the express network operated by Stagecoach Fife, and offered a fantastic degree of speed and comfort. *(Ewan Wood)*

A crisp winter's day finds Plaxton Premier-bodied Volvo B10M, L581HSG (581), sitting outside the shed at St Andrews awaiting the availability of its allocated stance. It will soon be making the journey to Edinburgh on the X59 limited stop service. As can be seen, the route of this service is displayed along the side windows of the coach. *(Ewan Wood)*

This is typical of the scene at St Andrews when there is a major golfing event taking place on the world famous old course. Thirteen Alexander-bodied Volvo Citybuses are lined up near the golf course, whilst employed on shuttle duties between St Andrews and Leuchars railway station. *(Ewan Wood)*

Alexander-bodied Mercedes minibus G281TSL (81), picks up a few passengers from the railway station bus interchange stop, at Leuchars. Situated just on the outskirts of the town, this location can look quite isolated, but is well served by passing bus services. *(Ewan Wood)*

Seen in St Andrews town centre in July 1993 is Alexander Y-type Leyland Leopard, XMS422Y (122). It is loading up with a few local before heading on a direct service 96 to Dundee. The board in front of the driver proudly displays 'Dundee (Direct) OAP's Welcome'. *(Malcolm Audsley)*

One of the Alexander-bodied T-type Leyland Leopards to survive into Stagecoach ownership was RSC190Y (290), seen in July 1993 making its way through the streets of St Andrews. By this time, the 'A' suffix letter after the fleet number denotes that it is a vehicle allocated to Aberhill, Leven, rather than the closed depot at Anstruther just down the Fife coast. *(Malcolm Audsley)*

Another one of St Andrews' allocation makes its way through the streets of Dundee in July 1998, at the start of its long journey back down the Fife coast on the service 95 to Leven. This is Volvo Citybus C800USG (920) was new in 1986 to Fife Scottish and ended its days, just recently, down south of the border. *(Malcolm Audsley)*

Tow wagon XXA854M (1054S) was former Alexander-bodied Leyland Leopard FPE54 in the Fife fleet. It was the tow vehicle allocated to St Andrews and is seen, shortly after being painted in the 'candy stripe' livery not long after Stagecoach took the over the helm in Fife. *(Malcolm Audsley)*

Alexander P-type-bodied Leyland Tiger, D522DSX (422S), seen making steady progress through the streets of St Andrews on a service 64 to Springfield, a few miles to the west of the town, in July 1993. It is not hard to see why these vehicles were nicknamed 'Portacabins'. *(Malcolm Audsley)*

This former Southdown Bristol VR was one of the buses that had been based in St Andrews for exclusive use on the local St Andrews tour. UWV617S (1107S) is seen on one of these tours on a dull-looking day with only a handful of sightseers on board. *(Malcolm Audsley)*

Another one of my 'ugly ducklings' – buses I think look weird – is the Carlyle-bodied Dennis Dart. In this instance it is in the shape of H71MOB (687), seen here trundling over the cobbled streets of St Andrews in August 2002. As I pointed out in *Kirkcaldy and Central Fife's Trams and Buses*, the body style reminds me of a snow shovel. *(Suzy Scott)*

M776TFS (76) was an Alexander-bodied Mercedes Benz Minibus. New in 1994, these buses did sterling work within Fife and were much used on the local services they were intended for. This one is seen on a local service 68 in Cupar during June 2002. It would appear to be a well patronised service at this time. *(Suzy Scott)*

R340HFS (340) is captured in February 2003 in St Andrews, vibrating on the cobbled street travelling through the town centre. It has just made the journey on the service 99B from Dundee and will terminate within a couple of minutes when it arrives in the town's bus station. The Volvo B10 with Alexander PS-type bodywork was a good combination and much loved by Fife drivers. *(Suzy Scott)*

Alexander-bodied Volvo Citybus C800USG (920) is seen here in February 2003 employed on a local service in St Andrews. It had obviously just completed a school run as the school bus boards are still on display, a practice not done nowadays. This vehicle was sold on to an operator down south shortly after being photographed. *(Suzy Scott)*

The former London, Northern Counties-bodied Volvo Olympian, has, over the last few years been the main double-decker type found in Fife. They were used extensively on school runs up and down the county and every depot had a good allocation of them. They are gradually being phased out but are still found, as exemplified here with two of the vehicles allocated to St Andrews. *(Brian McDevitt)*

Still very much in use when photographed in September 2012, one of the few remaining Volvo B10s with Alexander PS-type bodywork. These vehicles were work horses and very much regarded as stalwarts in the Fife fleet, as epitomised by R649LSO (20149), when seen in Stirling heading back on the arduous journey to St Andrews via Kinross. The journey times have changed little over the years, and it still takes almost two hours each way to complete the journey. (Chris Cuthill)

In keeping with the other bus station throughout Fife, St Andrews now has a modern, covered waiting room area. The stance layout is again to the modern practice of buses arriving 'nose in' on stance, this eliminates the need for passengers to cross over in front of other 'through' type bus operating areas. In this view, a trio of B7 coaches sit in their stances while employed on the various express services that St Andrews seems to enjoy. (Chris Cuthill)

Alexander Dennis Enviro300 SP59CTZ (27610) makes its way down Lady Wynd in Cupar. This was due to the Bonnygate being closed to help in the demolition of a local building. The Enviro300 is a good mid-range vehicle, used in a much similar way, on similar routes, as the old Leyland Leopards and Tigers would have been. *(Chris Cuthill)*

This is the rear end view of one of the more recent acquisitions for Stagecoach Fife. SP62BKF (28655) is a Scania chassis with standard-looking Alexander Dennis bodywork. These buses were introduced in autumn 2012 primarily for use on the service 99 between St Andrews and Dundee. *(Chris Cuthill)*

Fleet number 28655, is once again shown here in St Andrews on a return journey from Dundee on the 99B service. This is the front off-side view and clearly shows the Alexander Dennis style of body which nowadays unfortunately looks rather inherent with other types. *(Chris Cuthill)*

The former yard at Newburgh Depot is still used by Stagecoach as an out station, and various types of (usually) double-deckers can be seen parked up there. This view epitomises that clearly, as can be seen with the variety of chassis and body styles of show. *(Robert Clark)*

This former Central SMT Bristol FLF Lodekka, HGM335E, belongs to the Stagecoach Heritage Fleet and can often be found in the summer months on tours around St Andrews. It must have been a nostalgic trip for the elderly patrons seen leaving the bus at the end of their tour on a beautiful day at the end of August 2004. *(Michael Laing)*

Around the turn of the millennium, a batch of Alexander-bodied Volvo Olympians arrived in Fife from London. They were initially dual-doored and had a large type of London destination screen. They were quickly converted to single-door and had their destination screens replaced. R157VPU (16075) was allocated to St Andrews and is seen on a local service F1 in the town centre. *(Gordon Stirling)*

The service 95 is still going strong today and it regularly sees a bit of contrast with the vehicles used. Nowadays, anything from an Optare Solo to an Enviro400 can be found operating on this route as seen here with Optare SP06FND (47367) in April this year (2013). *(Chris Cuthill)*

Bringing us more or less up to date, SP61CWZ (54103) makes an imposing sight as it is seen arriving at St Andrews Bus Station on a service X59 from Edinburgh. These Plaxton-bodied, Volvo B13R's, were not without their early teething problems but have proved to be a winner with those looking to travel in style and comfort. *(Chris Cuthill)*